SCHIRMER PERFORMANCE EDITIONS

THE ROMANTIC ERA
Early Intermediate Level

Compiled and Edited by Richard Walters

AUDIO ACCESS INCLUDED
Recorded Performances Online

Recorded by

Alexandre Dossin
Matthew Edwards
Stefanie Jacob
Jennifer Linn
Margaret Otwell
Jeannie Yu

To access companion recorded performances online, visit:
www.halleonard.com/mylibrary

Enter Code
1855-9918-4834-7721

On the cover:
Réunion de famille (1867–68)
by Frédéric Bazille (1841–1870)

ISBN 978-1-4803-3826-5

G. SCHIRMER, *Inc.*

DISTRIBUTED BY

HAL•LEONARD® CORPORATION
7777 W. BLUEMOUND RD. P.O. BOX 13819 MILWAUKEE, WI 53213

www.musicsalesclassical.com
www.halleonard.com

CONTENTS

Though the table of contents appears in alphabetical order by composer, the music in this book is in progressive order.

The price of this publication includes access to companion recorded performances online, for download or streaming, using the unique code found on the title page. Visit **www.halleonard.com/mylibrary** and enter the access code.

The music in this collection has been edited by the compiler/editor Richard Walters, except for the pieces previously published in other volumes in the Schirmer Performance Editions series:

Gurlitt: March; Grandfather's Birthday
from *Gurlitt: Albumleaves for the Young, Opus 101*
edited and recorded by Margaret Otwell

Schumann: Sicilienne; Little Study; First Loss
from *Schumann: Selections from Album for the Young, Opus 68*
edited and recorded by Jennifer Linn

Tchaikovsky: The Doll's Funeral; At Church
from *Tchaikovsky: Album for the Young, Opus 39*
edited and recorded by Alexandre Dossin

COMPOSER BIOGRAPHIES
AND
PERFORMANCE NOTES

HERMANN BERENS
German composer, pianist, and teacher.
Born in Hamburg, April 7, 1826;
died in Stockholm, May 9, 1880.

Berens studied music first with his father, composer and flutist Karl Berens, and then with Karl Reissiger in Dresden before moving to Stockholm, where he would spend the rest of his life. There he was music director at an opera theatre, and professor of composition and piano at the Swedish Royal Academy of Music. Berens became known as a pianist and chamber musician. Though he composed music in various genres, Berens was primarily known for his piano music, some of which still remains on some syllabuses. Among his piano students was Queen Lovisa (Louise) of Denmark.

Piece in C Major
from *Fifty Piano Pieces for Beginners*, Op. 70, No. 32
The composer has provided no dynamic markings. Apparently, he did not add dynamics for any of the pieces in this set. We have made some suggestions about dynamics that may help you shape your performance. You may explore other possibilities, but do not make the mistake of playing the piece with no thoughtful plan for dynamics. The form is comprised of four phrases. The first phrase, A, is measures 1–4. The second, B, measures 5–8, is an answer to phrase A. Phrase C is a contrast, beginning in measure 9. In this section the moving eighth notes transfer to the left hand. Then in measure 13, there is a return of the A section, a repeat of the first phrase with a slight variation. The texture of the music is moving eighth notes against slow moving half notes. Notice that the eighth notes are slurred. There is a long phrase shaping both the moving eighth notes and the half-note accompaniment. This is not a piece to show off finger dexterity. Instead, it shows *legato* finger movement. There is an implied little melody in the right hand in the beginning, which includes the notes on the main beats (1 and 3) of the first few measures, then on beat 4 in measure 3. Something similar happens in the right hand in measures 5–8.

Probably the technical challenge to the student pianist is to play the eighth notes in the left hand in measures 9–12 with the same smooth legato as the eighth notes in the right hand elsewhere in the piece. The pianist on the companion recording has chosen a moderate tempo. One could imagine a tempo that is a bit quicker, but make sure that the tempo does not exceed your ability to play the eighth notes in the left hand smoothly and evenly.

FERDINAND BEYER
German composer and pianist.
Born in Querfurt, July 25, 1803;
died in Mainz, May 14, 1863.

Beyer was mostly revered as an arranger and transcriber of large orchestral works and operas for solo piano, a common type of arrangement in the nineteenth century when pianos were in nearly every middle class and upper class home. Apart from his arrangements, he published over 100 original works in a lighter vein. With the exception of the 106 pieces from the *Elementary Instruction Book*, which have become standard pedagogical studies and the basis for many other instructional works, Beyer's music is not widely known today.

Piece in G Major
from *Elementary Instruction Book*, Op. 101, No. 78
One of the challenges to the progressing pianist is to execute different articulations simultaneously. This little piece presents that challenge. We have recommended some articulation in brackets which seems organic to the music. You will notice in the main theme in measures 1–2 the right hand has bouncing staccato chords against a smooth left hand pattern. For independence of hands, it is highly recommended to practice the left hand separately, noting the smooth three-note phrase. There is a slight lift of the hand after each three-note phrase. In measure 9, in the left hand figure, the composer has asked us to sustain the principle note (on beats 1 and 4), which makes the middle section different in texture from what has preceded it. There is plenty of dynamic contrast possible in

this short work. We have suggested some dynamics, which seem to be implied and musically natural, in addition to what the composer has indicated. Notice in the right hand of measures 3–4 that the phrase marking covers two measures, rather than the short three-note phrase in the left hand. All of these articulation markings and phrasings will be clearest if this piece is performed without pedal; pedaling will blur the cleanliness of the phrasing. Notice in measures 1–2 that the fourth chord is slightly longer, allowing for a graceful end of the phrase. The bracketed *poco rit.* in measure 16 seems natural; a pianist might choose to save this *rit.* for the second time. The form of the piece is ABABA. The B section clearly begins in measure 9.

JOHANN FRIEDRICH BURGMÜLLER

German composer, pianist, and teacher.
Born in Regensburg, December 4, 1806;
died in Beaulieu, France, February 13, 1874.

The Burgmüllers were a musical family. Johann August Franz, the patriarch, was a composer and musical theatre director as well as the founder of the Lower Rhine Music Festival. Johann Friedrich's brother Norbert was a child prodigy at the piano and a composer. Johann Freidrich distinguished himself from his family by leaving Germany and establishing himself in Parisian circles as a composer of French salon music. Later in life he withdrew from performing and focused on teaching. As part of his teaching, he wrote many short character pieces for his students as etudes. Several collections of these are perennial favorites of piano teachers, especially the pieces from opus 100, 105, and 109.

Sincerity (La Candeur)
from *25 Progressive Studies*, Op. 100, No. 1
The form of the piece is AABB with a Coda. The A section is measures 1–8; the B section begins in measure 9 and repeats in measure 17. The end of the second B section in measure 24 leads into the Coda. There is eighth-note movement in almost every beat of the piece, carried by the right hand in section A. In section B there is alternation of the eighth-note movement between the two hands. Though the music has a finger exercise quality about it, the eighth notes should be played elegantly and smoothly. The harmony becomes colorful and surprising in measure 13 in the B section briefly, before resolving back to the tonic key. The title of the piece, "La Candeur" (Sincerity) is an indication not to take this music too rapidly. We suggest that the composer intends a purity

of spirit. It is not a show-off piece. Pedaling is required, but in this and all of Burgmüller's works, pedaling should be carefully considered. A change of harmony is a clue as to where to change the pedal. There is a natural phrase built into the music, sometimes indicated with "hairpins" (*crescendo* and *decrescendo* markings).

Ballade
from *25 Progressive Studies*, Op. 100, No. 15
There is an indication at the beginning of *misterioso*, which is an apt description of the sly and light, mischievous character of the music. Burgmüller has given us a narrative through the dynamic contrasts. If you adhere to what he has written, you will paint a colorful story that would not be inappropriate for Halloween night. This piece could be played without pedal. In fact, it is recommended that the pianist practice it with no pedal. The repeated accompaniment chords need to be crisp and light. Feel an easy bounce on the chords and avoid rigidity in the wrist and hand. The contrast between the phrased sixteenth notes against the short chords is essential to the character of the music. Almost throughout this ballade one hand is playing the accompaniment figure and the other hand is playing the melody. This is true at the beginning with the right hand playing the repeated chords, with the running melody in the left hand. At measure 19, the accompaniment takes over in the transition to the end of that section. The beginning of the new section occurs in measure 31; the melody has moved to the right hand. The composer adds a few chromatic notes in measure 47 to introduce a return to the minor key of the opening. Measures 57–86 are a repeat of the first section (measures 1–30). In measure 87, when the opening material returns, the composer surprises us. This section functions not as a reprise, but as a coda. Rather than having one hand play the melody and other the accompaniment, both play the melody together at *f*.

JEAN-BAPTISTE DUVERNOY

French composer and pianist.
Born c. 1802; died c. 1880.

Duvernoy published several hundred compositions during his life, usually arrangements of larger orchestral pieces or operas and many technical studies for pianists. Today he is best remembered for his *Elementary Studies*, Op. 176 and *The School of Mechanism*, Op. 120. Little is known about his life. There were other noted musicians and composers of nineteenth century France named Duvernoy.

Study in A Major
from *Elementary Studies*, Op. 176, No. 15
Many of Duvernoy's studies do not include dynamics, a common occurrence in educational etudes of the nineteenth century. We have suggested a few dynamics in brackets to help create a satisfying performance of this piece. It is in simple ABA form. Measures 1–8 are the A section; measures 9–16 are the B section; and we return to A in measure 17. One should practice primarily without pedal, noting the slurs and phrases that the composer has provided. Note the echo effect in measures 9–10 and measures 13–14. Though this piece is in a romantic style, it is somehow reminiscent of Mozart. There is a quiet nature to this music, and it should be played with grace and restraint. It will sound best with a refined touch, which comes from careful attention to tone and musical phrasing. As with any piece with an accompaniment figure in the left hand, it is essential to practice hands alone to make the accompaniment exactly executed, but quietly and elegantly.

ALBERT ELLMENREICH

German actor, director, writer, singer, and composer.
Born in Karlsruhe, February 10, 1816;
died Lübeck, May 30, 1905.

During his lifetime Ellmenreich was known mostly as an actor, playwright and theatre director, working in many cities in Germany. After many years of the touring life he retired from the stage in 1884. Ellmenreich was also an occasional composer of short character piano pieces, of which the "Spinning Song" has become an indispensable standard in international student repertoire.

Spinning Song
from *Musikalische Genrebilder*, Op. 14, No. 4
The title refers to someone working at a spinning wheel, spinning fibers into thread. Spinning songs were a common musical convention of the early Romantic period. The most famous is an art song by Schubert for voice and piano ("Gretchen am Spinnrade"). Ellmenreich's spinning song is happy and without conflict. The worker seems cheerfully content with the activity and enjoying her accomplishment. She is fluent and graceful at her task. The music is obviously in three large sections: B begins in measure 27; the return of A comes in measure 52. An important feature of the A section is the bouncing left hand figure.

There should be no pedal used, which would blur the accompaniment figure. The composer has written *leggiero* above the first right hand entrance, which is an indication to play with lightness. In measure 4 it is important to note the difference in articulation between the staccato eighth-note diad and the quarter-note diad. The final notes of this two-measure phrase are slightly longer and not clipped. Though it is not marked in the music, there is an implied hairpin swell over the two-measure phrase, occurring in measures 3–4, 7–8, and 9–10. The *p* in measure 15 is *subito* after the *f* in measure 14. Cleanly executing this sudden contrast will add crispness and wit to your performance. The tempo in the B section is the same as the opening section. This presents a completely different texture. The accompaniment moves to the right hand, with repeated chords. Because these chords are not marked staccato, they should be lightly played but not short and dry, possibly using pedal. Near the end of the B section, the melody moves to the right hand (measure 43). In measure 52 one might consider playing the return of the A section more quietly than at the opening of the piece. Notice that for the final measures the composer changes the left hand from staccatos to a phrased, smooth ending. Many student pianists have taken this famous piece too quickly. Note that *Allegretto* is an indication of a gentle speed, not racing ahead. The main quality for the entire piece is nimble gracefulness.

CORNELIUS GURLITT

German composer, organist, and pianist.
Born in Altona, February 10, 1820;
died in Altona, June 17, 1901.

Many of Gurlitt's piano works have colorful, descriptive names, no surprise given his lifelong interest in art. He studied music in Leipzig, Copenhagen, and Rome, where he was nominated an honorary member of the papal academy Di Santa Cecilia. His brother Louis was a very successful artist in Rome, and Cornelius himself studied painting for a time while living there. Gurlitt worked as a pianist and church organist, and also served as a military band master. He returned to his hometown of Altona, where the Duke of Augustenburg hired him as music teacher for three of his daughters. Gurlitt wrote symphonies, songs, operas, and cantatas, but he is best remembered today for his pedagogical keyboard pieces.

March (Marsch)
from *Albumleaves for the Young,* Op. 101, No. 1

This piece has a form of AABABA, which might seem complicated, but the music is straightforward. It is a happy little march, perhaps faster than a normal walking tempo. We have made editorial suggestions about articulation that help give the music bounce and character, and may help to create a successful performance. There is an implication of horns in the opening motive, which calls to mind a military band or call to arms. Be sure to note the slurs that connect the last note of measure 9 to the first note of measure 10; it is similarly executed in the next three measures. The piece should be played without pedal. A march needs a steady beat throughout, with no *rit.* at the end.

Grandfather's Birthday (Grossvaters Geburtstag)
from *Albumleaves for the Young,* Op. 101, No. 13

The character of this music is a combination of reverence and good humor. It is as if the scene is a procession, with children bringing presents to Grandfather with some tongue-in-cheek inflation of the importance of the procession. Grandfather is approached with great respect in the majestic chords of the introduction. Then the melody that begins in measure 5 shows childlike lightness. The little duet between the hands in measures 5–20 might be thought of as two children playing a duet for Grandfather, each on a melody instrument. The tune that enters in measure 5 is reminiscent of the nursery rhyme "Down by the Station," which may have its roots in German folksong. The chords in measure 21 (section B) seem an answer to the tune before and to the introduction. In the section that begins in measure 21, it might be helpful to think in two-measure phrases (measures 21–22, 23–24, etc., to measure 28). The three repeated notes in measures 29–31 seem to have some symbolic implication. Gurlitt has given us no real contrast in dynamics. Even though the composer has asked us to play loudly throughout, one should keep a buoyant touch so that the music dos not become rigid. The piece could be played with no pedal at all, or pedal could be added sparingly and judiciously. However, we recommend no pedal in measures 5–20.

STEPHEN HELLER

Hungarian pianist, composer, and teacher.
Born in Budapest, May 15, 1813;
died in Paris, January 14, 1888.

Heller begged his parents for piano lessons as a child. At the age of seven he was already writing music for a small band his father put together for him. The boy was sent to Vienna to study with Carl Czerny, but quickly found the lessons too expensive and instead studied with Anton Halm, who introduced Heller to Beethoven and Schubert. At the age of 13, Heller was giving concerts in Vienna as a pianist and two years later began touring Europe. His travels brought him in contact with Chopin, Liszt, Paganini, and most importantly Robert Schumann, with whom he developed a life-long friendship. Heller even contributed to Schumann's journal *Neue Zeitschrift* under the pseudonym Jeanquirit. After two years of touring, the rigorous schedule became too much for the boy and Heller settled first in Ausburg, and then in Paris to teach and compose. He wrote several hundred piano pieces, of which the short character pieces from opuses 45, 46, and 47 are frequently performed today.

Scampering from *25 Studies,* Book 1, Op. 47, No. 1

The act of scampering implies a lightness of movement. One cannot imagine an elephant scampering. This should be the primary clue as to what touch you should bring to this piece. The scampering here is of the most graceful variety. When we see constant movement of sixteenth notes, especially traded from hand to hand, as in most of this piece, it is musical challenge to make the sixteenth notes always even. It is very important for the left hand and the right hand to match one another precisely in touch, volume, and rhythm in this kind of figure, as if they are one unit. Practicing hands separately will reveal the constant presence of this two-note phrase in the left hand, with the first held through the second. The right hand answers it with an ingenious bit of harmonic suspension. The composer breaks the pattern in measure 15; the texture changes to sixteenth in the right hand and the rhythmic motion slows in measure 20. This allows the return of the opening material to sound fresh, with contrast before it. The return to the opening material is a deceptive recapitulation. Heller only gives us the first three measures of the opening before abandoning it and moving into a free variation to the end. Dynamically the music is predominantly of a quiet nature. It rises to *mf* but not beyond. Pedaling needs to be very carefully considered. If a pianist follows Heller's phrases explicitly, it would be easy to create a satisfying performance without any pedal at all. Like other master composers of piano miniatures (such as Schumann and Kabalevsky), Heller has completely composed every detail of articulation for the pianist. If one just pays attention to all details as marked, one can accomplish a very satisfying musical experience.

Berceuse from *25 Studies*, Book 2, Op. 47, No. 19
A berceuse is a lullaby. There are many types of lullabies. This one is faster than many, but the lullaby nature of it cannot be forgotten. Think of the music in longer phrases, not individual beats. One can imagine a rocking motion that would be typical of a lullaby. The biggest technical challenge is the accompaniment figure in the left hand. The composer asks for constant movement, which requires ongoing evenness. Any unevenness will be very exposed. Heller has marked this figure *legatissimo*, which means as smoothly as possible. The pianist will need to practice hands separately to attain a light, smooth touch in the left hand accompanying figure. Only after the left hand is mastered can we turn attention to where it belongs, which is the melody in the right hand. It should be shaped with graceful structure. When a romantic composer places staccato markings on a quarter note, such as measure 7, and also puts a slur above it, it is an indication to the pianist to phrase. Do not make the mistake of merely playing staccato chords without shaping the phrase. The entire piece is quiet, with the exception of short interruption in measure 25 with f. (Did the baby briefly cry out here?) The most difficult section of the music is measures 41–52, and will require extra special practice. Not only does the pianist need to keep the left hand accompaniment figure moving slowly and quietly, the right hand becomes more complicated, and with multiple voices. The only way to accomplish this type of section is to practice hands separately and slowly persistently, then move to hands together very slowly. Only after mastering a challenging section at a slow tempo should you gradually move to a performance tempo. Do not make the mistake of playing the most difficult section of this or any piece too aggressively. A typical student pianist tends to speed up at difficult sections and play with tension. Do not fall into this trap. Heller has given a complete script of details about dynamics, articulation and phrasing. There is not a question on any note in this brief piece as to what he intended. You must study all of these details and incorporate them into your interpretation. If you ignore dynamics, articulations, or phrasing, you are not playing the piece as the composer wrote it. The dynamics, articulations and phrasing are organically part of the composition, just as are the notes and rhythms.

THEODOR KULLAK
Prussian/German composer, pianist, and teacher.
Born in Krotoszyn, September 12, 1818;
died in Berlin, March 1, 1882.

One of the most influential piano teachers of the nineteenth century, Kullak began giving concerts at age eight, with the official support of the royal family of Prussia, and meeting with enthusiastic reception when performing for other royal courts. After briefly studying medicine in Berlin he moved to Vienna, where he studied with Carl Czerny. At the age of 25, he began to work for the Prussian court as a music instructor, and specialized in teaching royal children and youth for many years. Soon after, he cofounded what would become known as the Stern Conservatory in Berlin, and then the Neue Akademie der Tonkunst, which soon became the largest private music school in the country. Through this school, Kullak directly influenced thousands of pianists including Hans Bischoff, Moritz Moszkowski, Xaver Scharwenka, and Nikolai Rubenstein. Kullak's musical output was vast. Writing almost exclusively for the piano, he produced over 150 works, most of which were for students.

The Clock
from *Scenes from Childhood*, Op. 62, No. 2
It seems that Kullak means not just a clock but a race against the clock in this rapid piece. There is a happy quality to this dash, as if one is gleefully pursuing some goal, rather than being threatened by some ominous chase. There are many technical challenges. The pianist must move from crisply playing the same line in both hands in measures 1–8, to intricate melody and accompaniment in the left hand. The composer also asks for a variety of dynamics in this music, sometimes playing rapid notes loudly and sometimes softly. There is a tendency among student pianists to play too loudly when playing quickly, or to speed up when playing rapid rhythms. You will need to practice the section at measure 16 in order to move swiftly but at a soft dynamic. The sixteenth-note figures, such as in measures 4, 8, 20, 24, etc., are essentially written-out ornaments. The composer gives us a twist in the middle section in measure 17 by not having the hands together on these staccato eighth notes. It is very important to play staccato eighth notes like this evenly and crisply. You will create a dull performance if you do not observe Kullak's details of dynamic and articulations. All the articulation on the page, staccatos and slurs, should be accomplished through the fingers only. Certainly there should be no pedal used in the entire piece. Pedal would muddy the texture and articulations.. You will notice that the first section is repeated at measure 33 to the end.

KONRAD MAX KUNZ

German composer.
Born in Schwandorf, 1812;
died in Munich, August 3, 1875.

As a child Kunz played music with his father in taverns and festivals around Schwandorf. He studied theology before becoming first a choir director, then chorus director at the Royal Court and National Opera Theatre in Munich. Kunz is regarded as one of the founders of the tradition of male choruses in Bavaria, and wrote many choral pieces. He is remembered as the composer of the "Bayernhymne," the official anthem of Bavaria.

Canon in F Major
from *200 Short Two-Part Canons*, Op. 14, No. 95

Counterpoint is the combination of two or more melodic lines. This is a different texture from music that is built with a melody over accompaniment. Composers take many different approaches to composing counterpoint, such as in fugues and various imitative writing. A canon is the simplest form of counterpoint, with one musical voice imitating another. (A round is a canon and you certainly know a round, such as "Row, row, row your boat.") You will notice that the notes are not exactly repeated from one voice to the next in the canonic imitation. In the first statement the left hand plays C–F. The right hand answers F–B-flat. This is what is known as a tonal answer in the second canonic voice. Canons can be done this way. It is also quite common in a canon for the imitation to stop briefly, with the voices come together for a cadence, such as in measures 7–8. In the second section of the piece, which begins with the pickup to measure 9, the right hand leads and the left hand answers (again with a modified, tonal answer, not literal imitation). A musician playing a canon wants to make the musical imitation clear, so that the voices are clear to the listener. We have added some articulations such as slurs and staccatos that will add musical expression, instead of allowing the piece to sound like a technical, academic exercise.

THEODOR OESTEN

German composer.
Born in Berlin, December 31, 1813;
died in Berlin, March 16, 1870.

Oesten studied various instruments as a child before moving to Berlin at age nineteen, where he studied composition with several teachers. He became one of the most sought after piano teachers in Berlin. He became well known for songs and piano pieces in the sentimental German salon style of the period. Of his output of several hundred compositions, only a few are still performed today. One such is his *Mayflowers*, Op. 61.

Spanish Dance from *Mayflowers*, Op. 61, No. 10

It is interesting to note the player's point of view about any piece of music, as opposed to the listener's point of view. The listener is probably going to be drawn to the melody in the right hand, and certainly the musician wants to shape the melody and give it interest. However, as a player of this piece, the most important challenge is the left hand accompaniment figure. The composer has marked this staccato throughout. Here are the challenges: play the notes of each chord exactly together; play with absolutely even rhythm; play with consistent crisp touch; play with some buoyant bounce in the hand so that it does not become tense with rigidity; and make it an accompaniment supportive to the melody, but without calling undue attention to itself. If the left hand does not accomplish these things, and if it is not a steady bed of sound, any impact of the melody in the right hand will be negated. Regarding the right hand melody, articulation has been explicitly composed. Following the composer's articulations and phrasing you should be able to shape the melody in a lovely way. Executing the articulation exactly will require practice alone for the right hand, as well as the left hand. Do not forget the dance aspect of this music. Any dance requires steady rhythm for the dancer. Even though this is in a minor key, one could not in any way characterize this music as sad. Enjoy the playfulness of the piece.

CARL REINECKE

German composer, pianist, conductor, and teacher.
Born in Altona, June 23, 1824;
died in Leipzig, March 10, 1910.

Reinecke was taught by his father, the theorist J. P. Rudolf Reinecke, until he was sufficiently skilled at the piano to begin traveling through Europe. After spending some time at the court in Copenhagen and teaching at the Cologne Conservatory, he settled in Leipzig, where he befriended the musical leaders of the day, Felix Mendelssohn and Fanny Mendelssohn-Hensel, Robert and Clara Schumann, and Franz Liszt. Reinecke's fame as a performer and teacher eventually allowed him to become the director of the Leipzig Conservatory and the conductor of the Gewandhaus Orchestra. His 300 published compositions are in nearly every genre, including orchestral, opera, vocal, chamber works, and he also composed piano music for students.

Sonatina in G Major, Op. 136, No. 2

The musical form we know as a sonata became a characteristic of the Classical Era. A sonata is in multiple movements, which have certain formal characteristics. Composers of the Classical and early Romantic Era also wrote sonatinas, which were almost always for piano, and were abbreviated sonatas. Sonatinas were also almost always pieces written for piano students, as was the Reinecke Sonatina in G major. You will notice right away that the first and last movements are in G, but the middle movement is in C major. This is often the case with a multi-movement work, the middle movement is in a related key.

In the first movement, the composer has written an accompaniment figure of moving eighth notes in the left hand. This is to be played legato. The pianist will need to practice left hand alone to create a quiet, even figure. The right hand melody has the characteristics of a singer singing a melody. Some musicians even invent their own words when they have a particularly song-like melody, so they can create phrases as a singer would.

In the short minuet, the composer implies a two-note phrase in the first complete measure on beats 1 and 2. A pianist should try to taper this phrase slightly so that the second note is quieter than the first, but not in an extreme, exaggerated way. Using this approach of tapering to the end of the phrase takes taste and practice. If you exaggerate it, the listener will feel sea sick. This entire minuet is built of short phrases. This movement should be played without pedal except as marked by the composer in measures 17–19. Remember that a minuet is a courtly dance.

The Rondino means a miniature rondo, a musical form in which a theme returns again and again, with a variety of material between each occurrence of the theme. In this brief piece, the theme only returns once, but it is in the spirit of a rondo. The rondo is a common form for a third movement of a sonata or sonatina. Even though this movement is marked *vivace*, it should be played only as fast as you can gracefully accomplish it. The composer even states *con grazia* (with grace). Because

articulation has been very specially written by the composer, it is our opinion that this articulation and phrasing implies that no pedal should be used in this movement. Note that in measure 2, the quarter-note chord on beat 2 is not marked staccato; if you shorten it too much, you will make an unattractive end to the two-measure phrase. As with any fast music, a performer should practice slowly, both with hands apart and hands together, before attempting to master a quick tempo. There should be a pause after the first movement before beginning the second movement, and similarly after the second movement before beginning the third movement. The length of this pause is subjective and up to the performer. Do not rush the pause. Certainly your hands should come completely off the keyboard.

ROBERT SCHUMANN
German composer.
Born in Zwickau, June 8, 1810;
died in Endenich, July 29, 1856.

One of the major composers of the Romantic Era, Robert Schumann's short creative career gave the world major repertoire in symphonies, art song, chamber music and piano music. Besides being a composer, he was an accomplished writer about music, especially as a critic and then editor of the influential *Neue Zeitschrift für Musik*. He was married to concert pianist Clara Wieck, who championed his works after his death in 1856, the result of a severe struggle with mental illness. Schumann was an early supporter of the young Johannes Brahms. The *Album for the Young (Album für die Jugend)*, a collection of 43 short piano pieces, was composed in 1838 for Schumann's three daughters. Schumann made a specialty of short character pieces for piano, not entirely unrelated to his distinctive work as a major composer of art song.

Sicilienne (Sicilianish)
from *Album for the Young*, Op. 68, No. 11

A siciliana or a sicilienne was traditionally a slow movement in 6/8 in the Baroque Era. In that era, it was rather like a slow gigue or jig. By the Romantic Era of Schumann, the sicilienne had lost its Baroque characteristics, and composers sometimes used this label for pieces that tended to be in 6/8 and in the minor key. Schumann's sicilienne is almost like a rondo, meaning that a theme continues to reappear. Technically the form is AABBACABA. As you can see from that scheme, the A section, defined as the opening measures 1–8, continues to reappear. Schumann has given us an adjective as a tempo marking, *Schalkhaft*, which is translated as roguish. A rogue is a scoundrel. We think that what Schumann had in mind was mischief, which implies some wit and humor. Schumann was famous for writing character pieces, short miniatures that define a scene or a mood, or portray a person or event. The implied protagonist character in this music, it seems, plans mischief through measure 25, and the fast section beginning 26 is perhaps a scampering away from danger, or quick enacting of the mischievous plan. Even though this is a piece in minor key, there is a lightness about it. The composer has given us many details of dynamics and articulation to create a colorful, vibrant performance. It is recommend to learn this piece without any pedal. One might also choose to use no pedal in performance, which would be a valid choice. In the fast section, the most difficult technical challenges are the left hand quick changes of chords beginning in measure 31. It is very important to deliberately use carefully considered fingering to accomplish this. We have recommended a fingering that allows the hand to easily shift from chord to chord, but as with any fingering, find something that works for your hand. As with any fast music, a pianist must practice hands separately and at a slow tempo. Though Schumann gives us no articulation for most of the left hand chords in the fast section, a light touch is implied. One of the challenges in this piece is to make graceful transition from section to section, so that it sounds like a complete piece and not disjunct. The fermata at the end of measure 37 indicates a pause before the return to the opening music. There is an art to how long this pause should be, and how it should be part of the music. Experiment with different lengths of pause. Do not be afraid to wait a bit before moving on after the fermata.

Little Study (Kleine Studie)
from *Album for the Young,* Op. 68, No. 14
This little study is based on arpeggiated chords. In every measure of the piece, one could make a chord of all the notes within the measure. Schumann takes the harmony and makes an arpeggio, passing from the left hand to the right hand. Also, the left hand notes always move upward; the right hand answers by moving downward. Schumann tells the pianist at the top of the piece to play "lightly and very evenly." In playing arpeggios, it is usually the aim of a pianist to make all the notes of the arpeggio sound with

evenness, so that one note does not stick out. Also, rhythmic execution should be perfect, so there are no jitters disrupting the pattern. This takes technical practice. The only way that you will hear whether you are accomplishing absolute evenness is by practicing without pedal. Each measure of the piece is phrased, meaning there is a slight arc from the beginning of the measure to the end of the measure. This phrasing is accomplished naturally with the rising and falling of notes. You may choose to slightly emphasize the first note in the right hand of each measure, because there is an implied melody that this first right hand note constructs. When one begins to add pedal after much practice, it is important to understand the harmonic changes in each measure and to carefully make a pedal change on each new harmony. This usually happens on the downbeat of a measure. This piece needs to be played with gracefulness and a refined touch. There is room for interpretation regarding tempo. Since Schumann does not specifically tell us anything about the speed in his tempo marking, the best advice is to make sure the piece has a flowing quality.

First Loss (Erster Verlust)
from *Album for the Young,* Op. 68, No. 16
Schuman was known for creating short pieces which colorfully capture a mood. "First Loss" is such a piece. Since this is from *Album for the Young,* we can surmise that Schumann is talking about a child's first loss. This could be any event that creates an emotional abandonment. It could be a reaction to the breaking of a beloved doll or toy, or it could be something much more significant. However, whatever event precipitated this emotion, it was an important emotional loss for the child. Schumann only tells us "not fast." Certainly a sense of sadness needs to come through in performance. To accomplish this mood of sadness it is very important that pianist play very *legato* following the phrase markings the composer has given us. This sadness is interrupted twice, in measures 29–32 and measures 45 to the end. These sudden abrupt chords seem to be a rise of anger at what has happened. Regarding form, the first eight measures are repeated, with a different ending in measures 15–16. The section that begins with the pickup to measure 17 into measure 32 is repeated, beginning with the pickup to measure 33 to the end. We recommend that you practice without pedal, relying on the *legato* of the fingers to accomplish the smoothness of the music. In fact, one might choose to play the entire piece without pedal in a performance.

JEAN LOUIS STREABBOG
Belgian composer, pianist, and teacher.
Born in Antwerp, September 28, 1835;
died in Saint-Gilles, May 5, 1886.

Jean Louis Gobbaerts, successful for decades as a pianist and a piano teacher in Brussels, published over a thousand piano compositions under three different pseudonyms: Ludovic, Levi, and Streabbog (Gobbaerts spelled backwards). His music is largely forgotten, with the exception of a few light character pieces used as pedagogical exercises.

By the Seaside
from *Twelve Very Easy and Melodious Studies,* Op. 63, No. 7
Streabogg obviously has in mind gently flowing waves on the shore, musically represented by these gently rising arpeggiated figures. The eighth notes pass from left hand to right hand. A figure such as this, common in piano music, needs to be played with evenness both in the volume of each note and also in rhythmic precision. You don't want to do anything that disrupts the 8 eighth notes in a complete measure phrase. When music is built on patterns of eighth notes such as this piece, it is extremely important that the rhythm remain steady throughout. The music is in four sections: section A is measures 1–8; section B is measures 9–15; section C is measures 16–23; and the fourth section is a repeat of A, with variation in the final measures. There is a sudden f in measure 16 after a contained softness prior to that point. Streabogg may have had in mind a sudden dramatic rise in weather at this spot, but which quickly subsides. Practice should be without pedal. However, one should work up to a pedal change with each change of harmony. A recommendation would be to pedal on the downbeat of each measure. Pedal changes should be clear and not blurred. The pianist on the recording has taken a tempo on the moderate side of *allegro*. One could image this at a slightly faster tempo.

PYOTR IL'YICH TCHAIKOVSKY
Russian composer.
Born in Kamsko-Votkinsk, May 7, 1840;
died in St. Petersburg, November 6, 1893.

Tchaikovsky is the great Russian composer of the nineteenth century who achieved the most international success, and whose symphonies, ballets, operas, chamber music and piano music, continue to be a central part of the repertoire. Of his piano works *The Seasons*, Op. 37bis, *Album for the Young*, Op. 39, and his concerto are most familiar to present day pianists and teachers. *Album for the Young* was written in four days in May of 1878, with revisions later that year before publication in October. It was during this year that Tchaikovsky left his teaching post at the St. Petersburg Conservatory and began composing and conducting full time, a move made financially possible by the patronage of Nadezhda von Meck. Much of *Album for the Young* is inspired by folksongs, capturing observations and experiences from childhood in 24 fanciful miniatures.

The Doll's Funeral
from *Album for the Young,* Op. 39, No. 8
In their play many children begin to process the concept of death, an inevitable part of human experience. The doll's funeral communicates both a sense of playful melodrama and earnest mourning. The music is generally of a quiet, reverent nature. Tchaikovsky builds this piece in four-measure phrases. The first section, measures 1–16, is comprised of four such phrases. The contrasting middle section begins in measure 17. The composer continues the four-measure construction in measures 17–20 and measures 21–24. The harmonic motion of the music moves forward through the entire eight measures 25–32. The music rises to its most dramatic and loudest point at the climax of this phrase in measure 29. It is also the most chromatic and farthest away from the tonic key at this point. It is as if a rise of emotion occurs, and then the mourner gains control of his or her feelings to continue the solemn procession that begins with the return of the opening music in measure 33. One challenge in playing chords at the piano is to make certain all notes go down precisely together and that the harmony clearly changes as written. There is a funeral march quality to the music, as if the doll is being brought in procession to a backyard grave. A procession of this nature will be ruined if a pianist does not maintain a steady beat throughout.

At Church
from *Album for the Young,* Op. 39, No. 23
Tchaikovsky grew up in Russia, where the Russian Orthodox Church was predominant. The opening section, measures 1–12 and repeated in measures 13–24, sounds very much like a solemn Russian Orthodox hymn, a genre based more on modal than tonal harmony. To get in the spirit of this piece, one might seek out some liturgical music from the Russian Orthodox tradition. Because of

the repeated notes, one almost has the impression that Tchaikovsky has words in mind that he might be setting as part of his compositional inspiration. Because the first statement of the hymn (measures 1–12) begins softly, and the second statement begins *mf* in measure 13, the composer perhaps creates the impression that the music increases in volume as one approaches the church. The organ is also an implied presence in this music. After the two statements of the hymn tune, beginning in measure 25 the music feels almost like a long organ postlude. The low repeated E perhaps implies an organ pedal tone, over which the harmony changes. The texture of the music certainly changes in this second half. Because it is marked to be played very softly, this organ and chime music is perhaps heard from a distance. The harmonic changes beginning in measure 33 over the low bass note are particularly rich as the composer brings the chords from the high range down to the middle of the piano. The word *perdendosi* in measure 26 means dying away. Whatever this event, this is not a festive, happy celebration in this church service. Because of the mood of the music, we can assume it is an observance that is at least of a pondering nature or perhaps even something more solemn.

—Richard Walters, editor
Joshua Parman, assistant editor

Canon in F Major

from *200 Short Two-Part Canons*

Konrad Max Kunz
Op. 14, No. 95

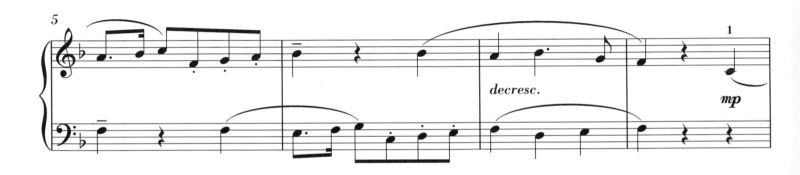

Fingering by Matthew Edwards.
The composer provided no tempo, dynamics, or articulations. These details are editorial suggestions.

Piece in C Major
from *Fifty Piano Pieces for Beginners*

Hermann Berens
Op. 70, No. 32

Fingering by Matthew Edwards.
The composer provided no tempo, dynamics, or articulations. These details are editorial suggestions.

The Doll's Funeral
from *Album for the Young*

Pyotr Il'yich Tchaikovsky
Op. 39, No. 8

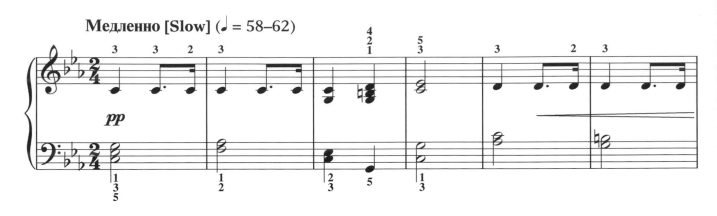

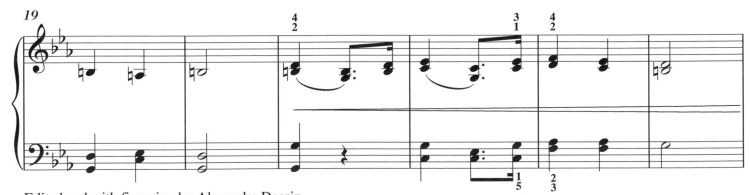

Edited and with fingering by Alexandre Dossin.
Tempo, dynamics, and articulations are original, by the composer.

At Church
from *Album for the Young*

Pyotr Il'yich Tchaikovsky
Op. 39, No. 23

Умеренно [Moderate] (♩ = 58–62)

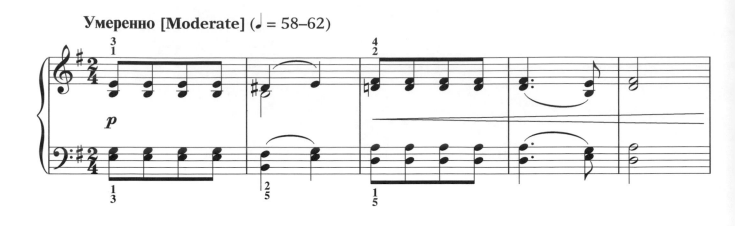

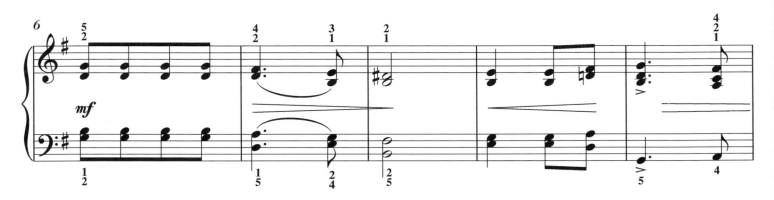

Edited and with fingering by Alexandre Dossin.
Tempo, dynamics, and articulations are original, by the composer.

Sincerity
(La Candeur)
from *25 Progressive Studies*

Johann Friedrich Burgmüller
Op. 100, No. 1

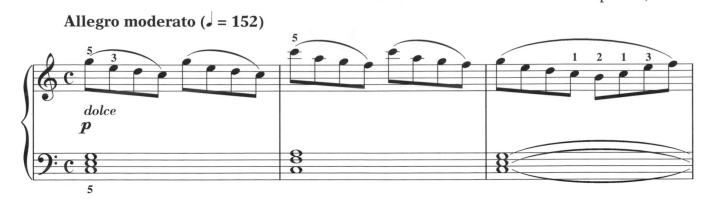

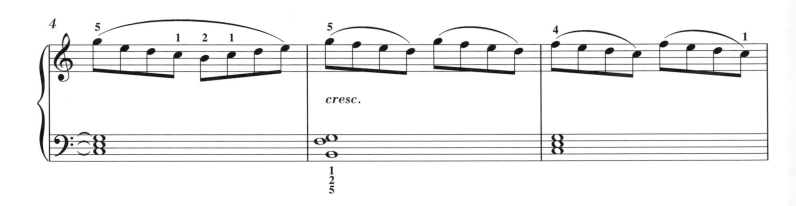

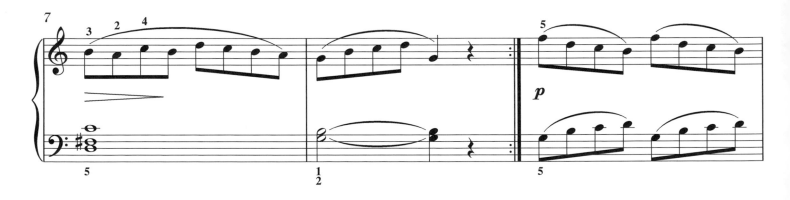

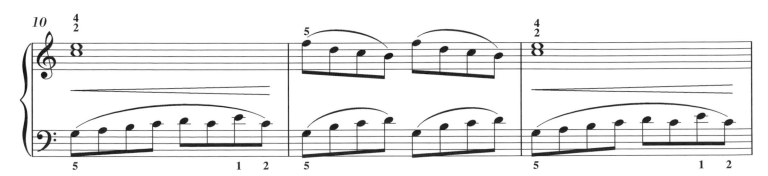

Fingering by Margaret Otwell.
Articulation and dynamics are as in the original edition.

By the Seaside
from *Twelve Very Easy and Melodious Studies*

Jean Louis Streabbog
Op. 63, No. 7

Fingering by Matthew Edwards.

Little Study
(Kleine Studie)
from *Album for the Young*

Robert Schumann
Op. 68, No. 14

Leise und sehr egal zu spielen
Lightly and very evenly

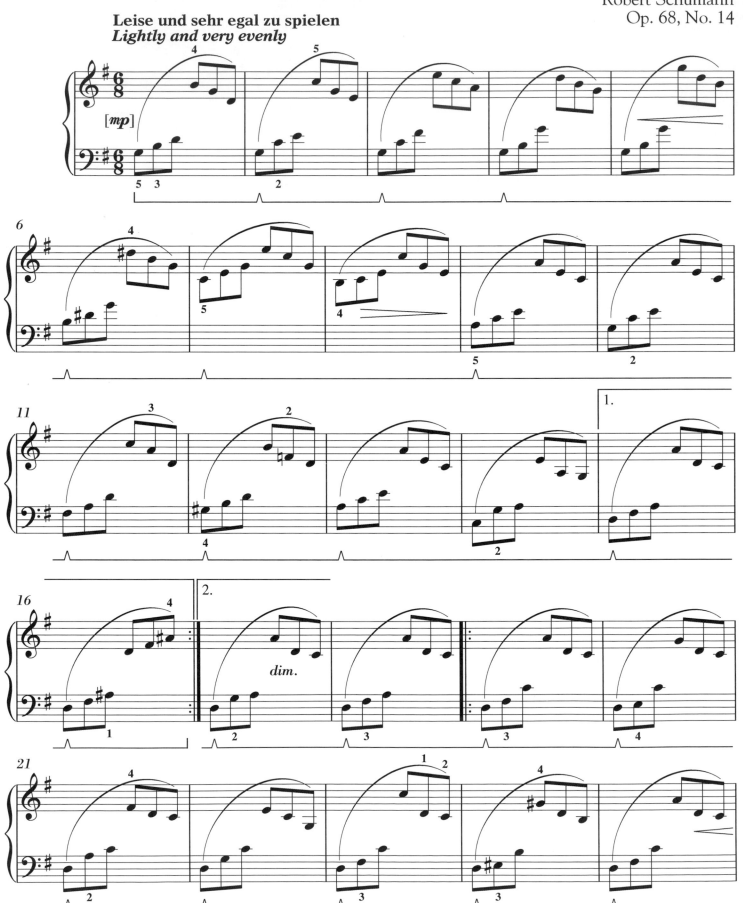

Edited and with fingering by Jennifer Linn.

* ossia

Grandfather's Birthday
(Grossvaters Geburtstag)
from *Albumleaves for the Young*

Cornelius Gurlitt
Op. 101, No. 13

Edited and with fingering by Margaret Otwell.

Spanish Dance

from *Mayflowers*

Theodor Oesten
Op. 61, No. 10

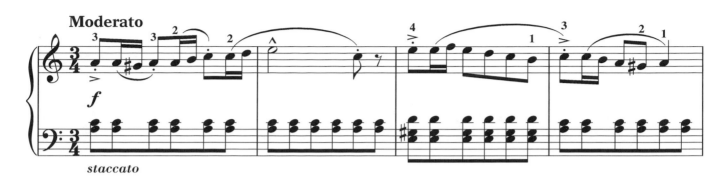

Fingering by Matthew Edwards.

Piece in G Major
from *Elementary Instruction Book*

Ferdinand Beyer
Op. 101, No. 78

Fingering by Matthew Edwards.
Editorial suggestions are in brackets.

Study in A Major
from *Elementary Studies*

Jean-Baptiste Duvernoy
Op. 176, No. 15

Fingering by Jeannie Yu.
Editorial suggestions are in brackets.

March

(Marsch)

from *Albumleaves for the Young*

Cornelius Gurlitt
Op. 101, No. 1

Vivace ma non troppo

Edited and with fingering by Margaret Otwell.
Articulations are editorial suggestions.

Scampering

from *25 Studies*, Book 1

Stephen Heller
Op. 47, No. 1

Fingering by Jeannie Yu.

Spinning Song

from *Musikalische Genrebilder*

Albert Ellmenreich
Op. 14, No. 4

Fingering by Stefanie Jacob.

Sicilienne
(Sicilianisch)
from *Album for the Young*

Robert Schumann
Op. 68, No. 11

Schalkhaft
Roguish

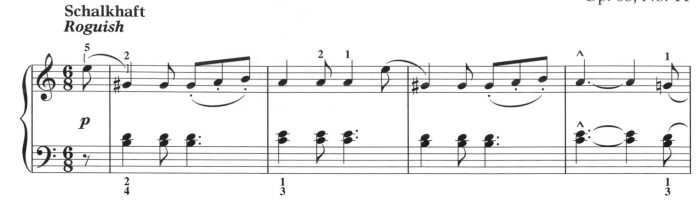

Edited and with fingering by Jennifer Linn.

Schluß
Fine

Schnell
Fast

Vom Anfang ohne Wiederholungen bis Schluß
From the beginning to Fine without repeat

Berceuse
from 25 Studies, Book 2

Stephen Heller
Op. 47, No. 19

Fingering by Jeannie Yu.

Ballade
from *25 Progressive Studies*

Johann Friedrich Burgmüller
Op. 100, No. 15

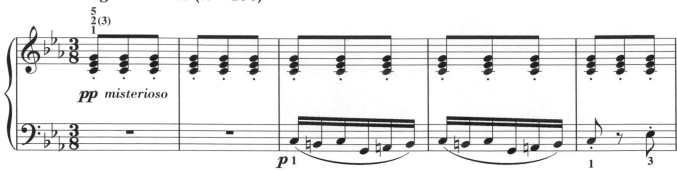

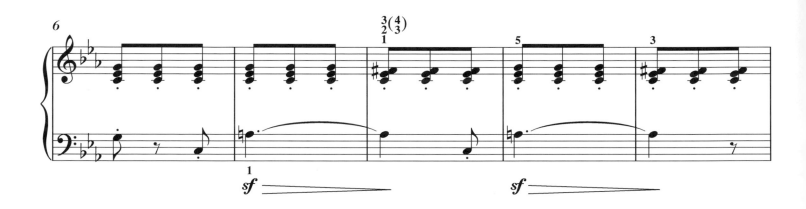

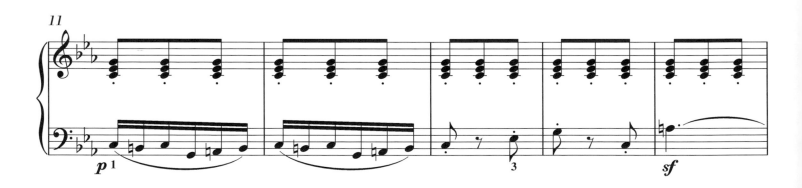

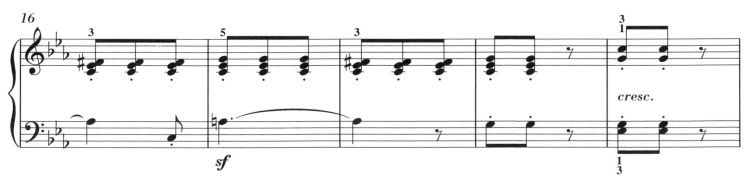

Fingering by Margaret Otwell.
Articulation and tempo are as in the original edition.

First Loss
(Erster Verlust)
from *Album for the Young*

Robert Schumann
Op. 68, No. 16

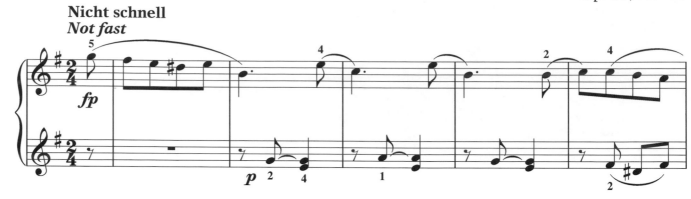

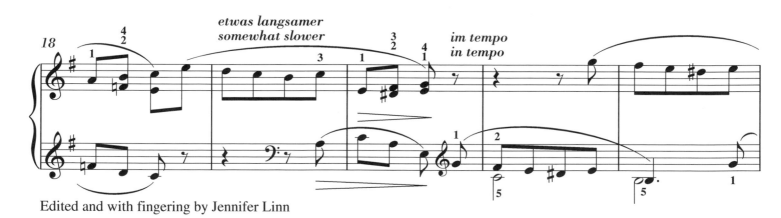

Edited and with fingering by Jennifer Linn

The Clock
from *Scenes from Childhood*

Theodor Kullak
Op. 62, No. 2

Allegro vivace

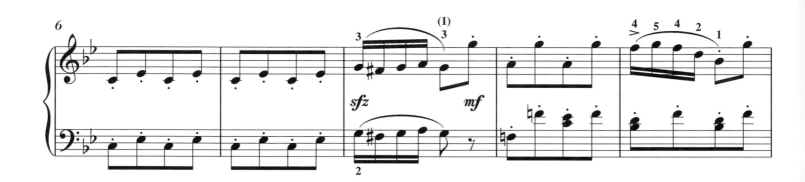

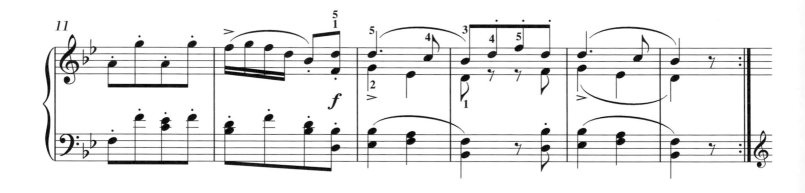

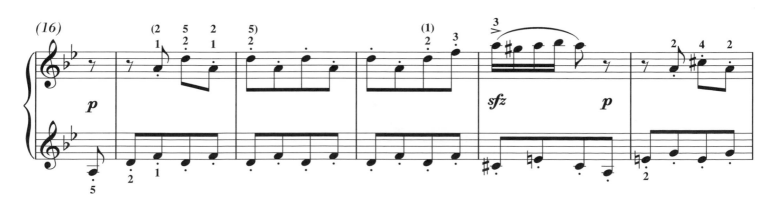

Fingering by Matthew Edwards.

Sonatina in G Major
I

Carl Reinecke
Op. 136, No. 2

Allegro moderato

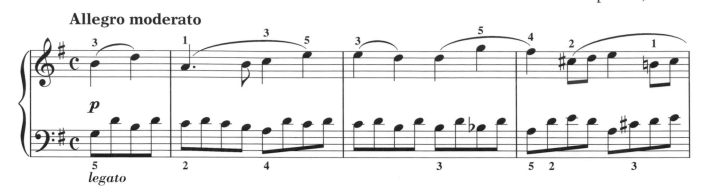

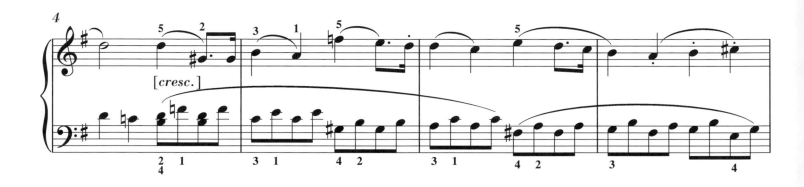

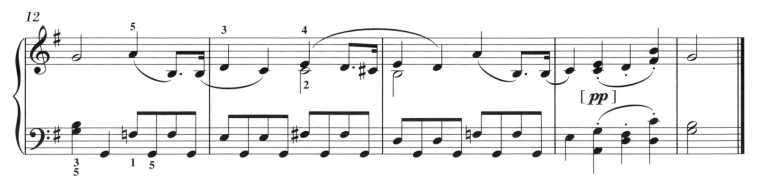

Fingering by Matthew Edwards.

II

MENUETTO

III

RONDINO

Vivace

ABOUT THE EDITOR

RICHARD WALTERS

Richard Walters is a pianist, composer, and editor of hundred of publications in a long music publishing career. He is Vice President of Classical Publications at Hal Leonard, and directs a variety of publications for piano, voice, and solo instruments. Walters directs all publishing in the Schirmer Performance Editions series. Among other piano publications, he is editor of the revised edition of *Samuel Barber: Complete Piano Music, Leonard Bernstein: Music for Piano*, and the multi-volume series *The World's Great Classical Music*. His editing credits for vocal publications include *Samuel Barber: 65 Songs, Benjamin Britten: Collected Songs, Benjamin Britten: Complete Folksong Arrangements, Leonard Bernstein: Art Songs and Arias, The Purcell Collection: Realizations by Benjamin Britten, Bernstein Theatre Songs, G. Schirmer Collection of American Art Song*, *28 Italian Songs and Arias for the Seventeenth and Eighteenth Centuries*, 80 volumes of standard repertoire in the Vocal Library series, and the multi-volume *The Singer's Musical Theatre Anthology*. Walters has published dozens of various arrangements, particularly for voice and piano, and is the composer of nine song cycles. He was educated with a bachelor's degree in piano at Simpson College, where he studied piano with Robert Larsen and composition with Sven Lekberg, and graduate studies in composition at the University of Minnesota, where he studied with Dominick Argento.